Let Freedom Ring

The Underground Railroad

Bringing Slaves North to Freedom

by Judy Monroe

Consultant:
Debra Jo Laveck
Northeast Regional Coordinator
for the Friends of Freedom Society
Ohio Underground Railroad Association
Ashtabula, Ohio

Bridgestone Books
an imprint of Capstone Press
Mankato, Minnesota

Bridgestone Books are published by Capstone Press,
151 Good Counsel Drive, P.O. Box 669, Mankato, Minnesota 56002.
www.capstonepress.com

Printed in the United States of America

Library of Congress Cataloging-in-Publication Data
Monroe, Judy.
    Underground Railroad : bringing slaves North to freedom / by Judy Monroe.
      v. cm.—(Let freedom ring)
    Includes bibliographical references and index.
    Contents: Escape from slavery—Slavery in America—The Underground Railroad begins—On the Underground Railroad—Stories of Courage—The Underground Railroad Ends.
    ISBN 0-7368-1344-6 (hardcover)
    ISBN 0-7368-4521-6 (paperback)
    1. Underground railroad—Juvenile literature. 2. Fugitive slaves—United States—History—19th century—Juvenile literature. 3.Antislavery movements—United States—History—19th century—Juvenile literature. [1. Underground railroad. 2. Fugitive slaves. 3. Antislavery movements.] I. Title. II. Series.
E450 .M76 2003
973.7'115--dc21
                                                                       2002002570

Editorial Credits

Bradley P. Hoehn, editor; Kia Adams, series designer; Juliette Peters, book designer; Erin Scott/SARIN Creative, illustrator; Kelly Garvin, photo researcher; Karen Risch, product planning editor

Photo Credits

"Harriet Tubman's Underground Railroad" by internationally acclaimed artist Paul Collins, Paul Collins Fine Art, Michigan, cover; Stock Montage Inc., 5, 23, 37; Hulton Archive by Getty Images, 9; The Maryland Historical Society, Baltimore, Maryland, 11, 14; Library of Congress, 12-13, 18, 30-31, 39, 40-41, 42; The Jackson Homestead, Newton, Massachusetts, 17; Capstone Press/Gary Sundermeyer, 21; Ohio Historical Society, 25, 27; Unicorn Stock Photos, 28-29; Bettman/Corbis, 33; Stock Montage Inc./The Newberry Library, 34, 43; Corbis, 36.

3   4   5   6   07   06   05

Table of Contents

Features

Chapter One

Escape from Slavery

The "Underground Railroad" was the term given to slave escape routes. The Underground Railroad was an informal network operated by people opposed to slavery. These people helped runaway slaves reach safety in Northern states or in Canada. Slavery was illegal in Canada. Underground Railroad routes led from the South to the North.

The Underground Railroad was never formally organized. It sprang up and grew over time as more people helped runaway slaves move to the North. The Underground Railroad was most active from 1830 until the outbreak of the U.S. Civil War (1861–1865).

It was against the law to help runaway slaves. Many people, African American and white, slave and free, helped make the Underground Railroad possible. They helped slaves because they believed that no person should own another person.

Slaves often were hunted down while trying to escape. Slaves sometimes were beaten or even shot when captured. It was against the law to help runaway slaves.

How the Underground Railroad Got Its Name

No one knows how the term "Underground Railroad" started. The growing railroad network in the United States made it easy for people to use terms like "conductor" as a code for the Underground Railroad. No matter how the term began, the Underground Railroad quickly grew. It proved to be a successful passageway for many runaway slaves.

Some people believe the term Underground Railroad began in the 1770s. A slave named Tice Davids ran away from his master's farm in Kentucky. Davids ran to the Ohio River. He jumped in and swam to the far side of the river. He came out at the slavery-hating town of Ripley, Ohio. A white man hid Davids in the basement of his house. Davids' master followed but could not find him in Ripley. The man told everyone that Davids must have gone onto an "Underground Road."

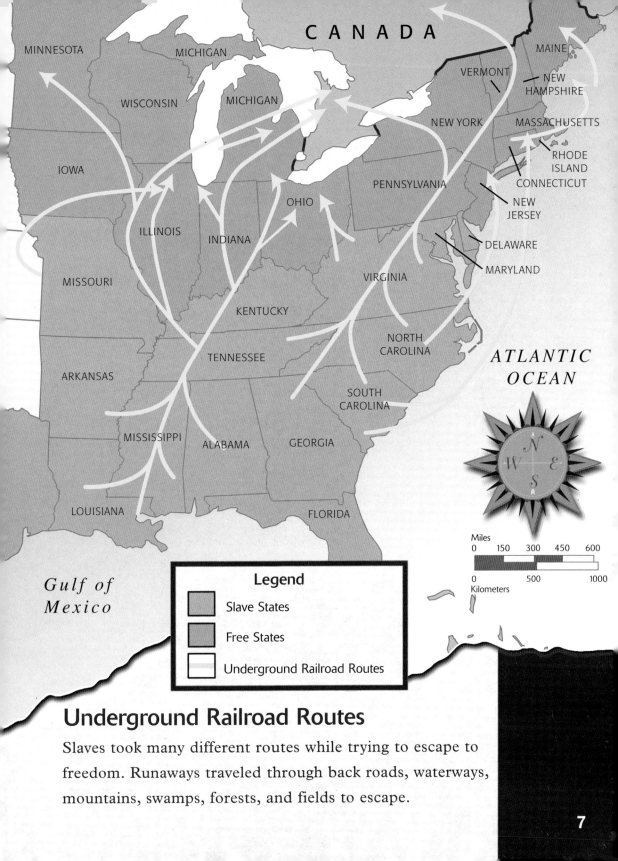

CANADA

MINNESOTA

MICHIGAN

MAINE

WISCONSIN

MICHIGAN

VERMONT

NEW
HAMPSHIRE

IOWA

NEW YORK

MASSACHUSETTS

PENNSYLVANIA

RHODE
ISLAND

CONNECTICUT

ILLINOIS

INDIANA

OHIO

NEW
JERSEY

DELAWARE

MISSOURI

VIRGINIA

MARYLAND

KENTUCKY

ATLANTIC
OCEAN

ARKANSAS

TENNESSEE

NORTH
CAROLINA

MISSISSIPPI

ALABAMA

GEORGIA

SOUTH
CAROLINA

LOUISIANA

FLORIDA

*Gulf of
Mexico*

N
W E
S

Miles
0   150   300   450   600

0   500   1000
Kilometers

Legend

Slave States

Free States

Underground Railroad Routes

Underground Railroad Routes

Slaves took many different routes while trying to escape to
freedom. Runaways traveled through back roads, waterways,
mountains, swamps, forests, and fields to escape.

7

Chapter Two

Slavery in America

Beginning in the 1500s, slave hunters sailed to Africa and took men and women as prisoners. They chained the prisoners to each other and forced them to walk many miles to the coast. Sick or weak people were left behind to die.

At the coast, the remaining prisoners often were branded with a hot iron. They were locked into dungeons. The traders then packed the prisoners into ships bound for the American colonies.

The trip to North America lasted six to ten weeks. Many African prisoners died from disease while on the ship. Those who made it through the trip were sold as slaves to people throughout the colonies.

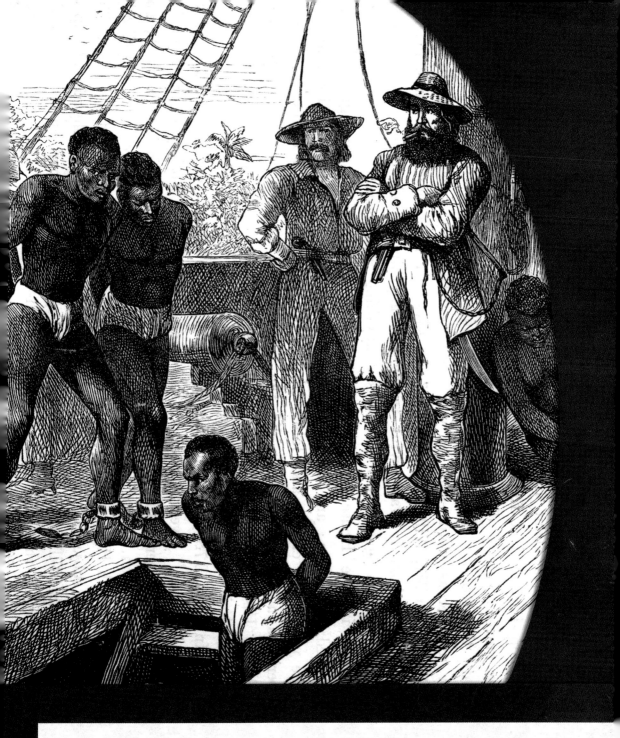

Slaves were forced aboard ships sailing to the American colonies. Prisoners were chained and put below in the hold of the ship.

Free No Longer

The colonists first recognized Africans as indentured servants. These servants agreed to serve a master in America for a set time, usually seven years. Poor Europeans worked in the colonies the same way. In 1619, the first African indentured servants arrived in Jamestown, Virginia. Very few Africans were considered indentured servants.

In 1641, Massachusetts passed a law that allowed slavery of Africans. The law considered all indentured servants to be slaves. In 1660, Maryland and Virginia passed similar laws. New laws allowed whites to enslave Africans for life. A child born to an African slave remained a slave for life. By 1755, all 13 colonies had slavery laws.

Slaves in the South

Southern farmers could grow and harvest more crops using slave labor. Large farms called plantations sprang up in the South. Farmers grew crops such as cotton, tobacco, rice, sugar, and indigo. Indigo is a plant used to make blue dye. Slaves cleared the land and planted, tended, and harvested the crops.

Many slaves lived and worked in terrible conditions. They often did not get enough to eat. They lived in small, shabby log or board cabins. They sealed cracks in the cabin walls with mud. The floors were made of dirt. Sometimes 15 or more slaves lived in these drafty places. Slaves on richer plantations did not necessarily eat better. Because

Slaves quarters were often in horrible shape. The floors of the houses were dirt and the walls were sealed with mud or clay to keep out the rain and cold.

there were more slaves, there was more competition for the food.

Most slaves worked from dawn until after dark. The hard work, poor living conditions, and unhealthy diet led to diseases and tooth decay. Many slaves had rotten or missing teeth. They often had coughs and were sick with influenza, an illness that causes high fevers and muscle pains.

Many slave owners punished slaves for any type of misbehavior. Slaves were beaten, bound in chains, or starved for even small deeds such as talking back or working too slowly. Runaways who

Slave cabins often housed more than one family. Slaves often lived in horrible conditions. They received a monthly allotment of cornmeal and little else to eat.

Slave Meals

Most slaves often ate the same types of foods day after day. Their owners gave them cornmeal, salt pork, and sometimes molasses. If the slave holders had extra food, slaves might receive small amounts of fresh vegetables or fruit. Some slaves were allowed to have small gardens to grow their own food.

were caught received beatings so severe that many died. Death was often the punishment for slaves who committed murder, robbery, or who started fires or rebellions.

Slaves could live together as husband and wife, but the laws of few colonies considered them legally married. Masters often separated husbands and wives when they sold them to new owners. Children sometimes were sold from their families, never to see them again.

Protest by Slaves

Some slaves protested their cruel treatment. They destroyed or stole property. Some rebelled by faking illness or injury. Some tried killing themselves. Some slaves ran away by themselves. Some bands of mostly male fugitive slaves, lived in swamps and mountains to avoid being captured. Others, like the group pictured below, ran away in groups called maroons.

African Americans in the North

Fewer slaves lived in the North than in the South. Some worked on farms and grew crops or tended to cattle and sheep. These farms were much smaller than Southern plantations.

Slaves living in Northern cities worked for their owners in many ways. They became carpenters, tailors, bakers, blacksmiths, and furniture makers. Some learned to read and write. Slaves were sometimes mistreated by their owners. Slave owners beat slaves or withheld food for periods of time as punishment for misbehavior.

After the American Revolutionary War (1775–1783), Vermont freed its slaves. Pennsylvania and other Northern states soon freed their slaves, as well.

Some whites discriminated against free African Americans in the North. Former slaves did not have the same access to education and jobs. They often were not allowed to talk or eat with whites. In some states of New England, free African Americans could vote. But in other Northern states, they could not.

Chapter Three

The Underground Railroad Begins

No one knows exactly when the Underground Railroad started. Historians believe it began in the 1770s. But antislavery movements started as early as the mid-1600s.

Growth of Antislavery Movements

In 1652, a group of Quakers in New England spoke against holding African Americans as slaves. Quakers were members of a religious group that believed all people should be equal.

In 1758, Quakers in Philadelphia voted to keep slaveholders out of their religious group. Soon, Quakers in other states followed their example. In 1775, Anthony Benezet of Philadelphia began the world's first abolitionist society. Abolitionists wanted to end all slavery. Similar abolitionist societies soon sprang up across the United States.

In 1846, these people were an abolitionist family. They believed slavery was wrong and helped runaway slaves escape to freedom.

Slavery Laws

The U.S. Congress passed several laws regulating slavery. The first was the Fugitive Slave Law of 1793. This law declared that fugitives, or runaways, were property and should be returned to their owners. Slave owners had the right to seize their runaway slaves in any state. The law also declared that helping runaway slaves or preventing their capture was a crime. Many people in the North ignored this law. Several states passed laws that did not allow government officials to help capture runaways.

Posters offering rewards for runaway slaves were common in the late 1700s and early 1800s. Owners often relied on slave hunters to return slaves who tried to escape.

$200 Reward.

RANAWAY from the subscriber, on the night of Thursday, the 30th of Sepember.

FIVE NEGRO SLAVES,

To-wit: one Negro man, his wife, and three children.

The man is a black negro, full height, very erect, his face a little thin. He is about forty years of age, and calls himself *Washington Reed*, and is known by the name of Washington. He is probably well dressed, possibly takes with him an ivory headed cane, and is of good address. Several of his teeth are gone.

Mary, his wife, is about thirty years of age, a bright mulatto woman, and quite stout and strong.

The oldest of the children is a boy, of the name of FIELDING, twelve years of age, a dark mulatto, with heavy eyelids. He probably wore a new cloth cap.

MATILDA, the second child, is a girl, six years of age, rather a dark mulatto, but a bright and smart looking child.

MALCOLM, the youngest, is a boy, four years old, a lighter mulatto than the last, and about equally as bright. He probably also wore a cloth cap. If examined, he will be found to have a swelling at the navel.

It is supposed that they are making their way to Chicago, and that a white man accompanies them, that Washington and Mary have lived at or near St. Louis, with the subscriber, for about 15 years.

A reward of $150 will be paid for their apprehension, so that I can get them, if taken within one hundred miles of St. Louis, and $200 if taken beyond that, and secured so that I can get them, and other reasonable additional charges, if delivered to the subscriber, or to THOMAS ALLEN, Esq., at St. Louis, Mo. The above negroes, for the last few years, have been in possession of Thomas Allen, Esq., of St. Louis.

ST. LOUIS, Oct. 1, 1847.

WM. RUSSELL.

The British Promise to Free Slaves

Great Britain needed soldiers during the Revolutionary War. The British promised freedom to American slaves who fought for them. Thousands of slaves fled from their owners and went to help the British.

When Britain lost the war, Americans demanded the return of their slaves. Some runaways went back into slavery. Many of these free slaves had to leave the United States, or their owners could recapture them. Some former slaves moved to Canada. Others sailed to West Africa.

In 1850, Congress passed a second and stronger Fugitive Slave Act. Any people who helped runaways could be arrested, put into prison, or charged heavy fines. This law allowed owners to hunt for suspected runaway slaves anywhere in the United States. Some slave owners hired slave hunters to find their runaway slaves. Slave hunters and slave holders also used dogs to hunt for runaways. Professional slave hunters sometimes turned in free African Americans, claiming they were escaped slaves.

Other religious groups began to speak out against slavery. The Methodist Church told its members that they could not buy or sell men, women, or children as slaves. The Presbyterian Church split on the issue of slavery. Many abolitionist Congregational churches formed as a result of this split. In 1847, an antislavery church was founded in Ripley, Ohio. The members of this religious group built new churches and carried their message to other states.

Slave Uprisings Raise Awareness

Slave uprisings helped bring awareness of the issue of slavery to the public. Newspapers wrote about some of these uprisings. On August 30, 1800, Gabriel Prosser and a group of 1,000 slaves planned to attack Richmond, Virginia. Prosser planned to take the governor hostage. He believed that if the slaves fought for their rights, poor white people would join them. A huge thunderstorm stopped the uprising. Their plan was discovered, and Prosser and 15 of his men were hanged.

Uncle Tom's Cabin

In 1852, Harriet Beecher Stowe wrote *Uncle Tom's Cabin*. The book sold very quickly. It told the story of two slaves. One escaped by the Underground Railroad and the other was abused by his owner. Readers were upset to read of the ill-treatment of slaves, and many people joined the abolitionists. Many readers first learned about the Underground Railroad from reading this book.

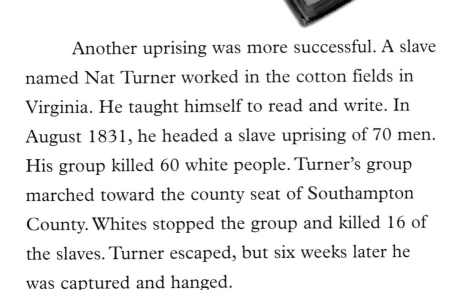

Another uprising was more successful. A slave named Nat Turner worked in the cotton fields in Virginia. He taught himself to read and write. In August 1831, he headed a slave uprising of 70 men. His group killed 60 white people. Turner's group marched toward the county seat of Southampton County. Whites stopped the group and killed 16 of the slaves. Turner escaped, but six weeks later he was captured and hanged.

The Abolitionists

Abolitionists used many methods to end slavery. They wrote about their cause in books, pamphlets, and newspapers. Some spoke at public meetings.

Abolitionists did not always agree on the best way to end slavery or the best way to help runaway slaves. Many believed that money and energy should go to political action.

Abolitionist David Walker was a free African American who wanted to help runaway slaves. In 1829, he wrote a 76-page antislavery booklet. He told slaves to run away because their time to be free was coming. Few slaves could read, so the message was mostly read by abolitionists. The booklet sold well and was carried to the slave states. It also helped to increase antislavery feelings in the North.

Antislavery Movement Gains Popularity

Lucretia Mott was a Quaker who helped organize women's abolitionist organizations. These groups of white and African American women held antislavery lectures, organized fairs to raise money, and started schools for African American children.

Antislavery societies soon became popular across the nation. By 1840, more than 1,000 antislavery societies existed across the United States.

In 1847, Frederick Douglass began to publish the *North Star*, an abolitionist newspaper. Douglass, once a slave, was one of the most popular speakers for abolition. Douglass published the *North Star* until 1860.

William Lloyd Garrison was an abolitionist. On December 4, 1833, he met with 63 people in Philadelphia. The group agreed in writing that its members would do everything possible to end slavery. Women attended the meeting, but they could not sign the agreement.

Chapter Four

On the Underground Railroad

At the end of the War of 1812 (1812–1814), U.S. soldiers spread the word that Canada was a safe land for runaways. Some slaves began the long and difficult journey north. Fugitive slaves turned to the Underground Railroad for help.

Dangers

A huge network of homeowners hid runaways and guided them from one safe place to another. Slaves had to stay ahead of the slave hunters who wanted to capture them. They also had to stay out of sight.

Runaway slaves faced great dangers traveling to the North. If caught, they often were beaten and their wounds were washed with salt and water to cause them further pain. Sometimes slave owners cut off fingers or toes as punishment for running away.

This former slave stood at the start of a trail used by runaway slaves. The trail led to the John Rankin House in Ripley, Ohio. It was a stop on the Underground Railroad.

War of 1812 and Runaway Slaves

In 1812, the United States started a war with Great Britain by attacking the British colony of Canada. The War of 1812 began because the British interfered with United States trading shipments. The British offered land and freedom to African Americans if they would fight for the British. Nearly 2,000 African Americans, mostly escaped slaves, joined the British forces. The African Americans who fought for Britain remained free.

In 1819, the U.S. government asked Canada to find and return any slaves who had fled to Canada. The Canadians refused to help but did allow U.S. citizens to recover their slaves at that time. In 1833, Great Britain passed the Slavery Abolition Act. This law ended slavery throughout Great Britain and its colonies, including Canada. Slave hunters were no longer allowed to enter Canada. Any escaped slaves living there were now free.

People who led the runaways to safe hiding places were called "conductors." The hiding places were called "stations," and the escaped slaves were called "passengers." People called "stationmasters" took in runaways and helped them move to their next place of safety. The final destination for the passengers was Canada or the Northern free states. After 1833, Canada did not tolerate slavery and did not allow slave hunters to enter that country.

Escape

Escape from a slave owner was difficult. Slaves had to carry written permission whenever they left their owner's home. They sometimes could not ride trains or cross bridges without written passes. Carrying food or clothing suggested that a slave was running

Uncle "Billy" Marshal was a conductor of the Underground Railroad in Ripley, Ohio.

away. Most runaways traveled by night to avoid being seen. They rested and hid during the day. They carried little clothing or food and often found or stole food along the way.

There were dozens of Underground Railroad routes. Some took slaves to free states such as Pennsylvania, Massachusetts, and New York along the East Coast. In the Midwest, the routes led to Ohio, Indiana, and Michigan.

Runaway slaves often hid on rural farms like this one. They traveled by night and hid in the barns during the day.

Hiding Places

Hiding places included houses, farms, barns, caves, and secret compartments. Sometimes graveyards served as hiding places. Cemeteries were often located close to rivers and placed just outside of towns or nearby churches.

Runaway slaves usually walked, guided only by the North Star. By following the North Star, runaways knew they were headed in the right direction. On cloudy starless nights, they used tree moss as a guide. Moss grows on the north side of tree trunks.

Runaways traveled through back roads, waterways, mountains, swamps, forests, and fields to escape. In later years, they sometimes traveled by wagon, steamship, boat, and even railroad trains.

Many runaways came from the upper Southern states. They were usually young, unmarried adult men. It was unusual and dangerous for families to escape together. Escaping slaves looked for safe houses in towns or on farms where free African Americans or abolitionists could hide them. Conductors met them at these points.

Secret Codes

People who worked on the Underground Railroad often used secret codes to let runaways know when travel was safe. Some songs contained codes. One song told listeners to "Follow the Drinking Gourd." The Big Dipper is a constellation of stars shaped like a water dipper or a drinking gourd. The handle of the dipper points to the North Star. Other songs such as "Swing Low, Sweet Chariot," and "Go Down Moses" carried coded messages related to escape.

Ordinary household objects often were used as coded directions. A family might hang a quilt out a window or on top of a fence to air. The pattern of a particular quilt might be a signal. A bear claw pattern might mean slaves were to follow bear tracks over the mountains. The four diamonds of the crossroad pattern told travelers to head for Cleveland, Ohio. This city was a crossroads on the Underground Railroad. Another quilt called the drunkard's path indicated that the best way north was not always straight. A quilt with a house and smoking chimney told slaves that they were by a safe house.

Tapping stones together signaled to runaways that it was safe to come out of hiding. Runaways were given codes to use as they traveled along the Underground Railroad. They learned secret knocks and passwords to use as they passed from safe house to safe house.

A quilt like this bear claw pattern hanging on the porch was a sign for runaway slaves. The pattern told runaways to follow bear tracks to escape over the mountains.

Chapter Five

Stories of Change

People who conducted the Underground Railroad took great risks. Many people disliked abolitionists and wanted them killed. People who helped runaway slaves had to do so in secret. Helping runaway slaves was against the law.

Stories of Runaways

Frederick Douglass was about 20 years old when he ran away from his owner in Maryland. He got false papers that said he was free. He disguised himself as a sailor and took a train to Philadelphia. He settled in New York City. Douglass then opened his home to runaways on the Underground Railroad.

Eliza Harris was a Kentucky slave. After two of her children died, she heard her owner planned to sell her last child. She was determined not to let such a thing happen. One night she grabbed her 2-year-old son and left. Months later, they made it to Ohio.

THE FUGITIVE'S SONG,

Frederick Douglass was a runaway slave who became a conductor on the Underground Railroad. "The Fugitive's Song" was an antislavery tune about runaway slaves on their way to freedom.

Box Hiding Places

Clarissa Davis dressed as a man and hid in a box on a ship in Portsmouth, Virginia. She safely reached the free North with help from the Underground Railroad conductors.

Henry Brown escaped from Virginia inside a mailing crate. He traveled upside down for 26 hours to Philadelphia. There, he was safely delivered to the Antislavery Society. Henry was forever known as Henry "Box" Brown. He became a popular abolitionist speaker.

In 1844, Lewis Hayden escaped slavery with his wife and son. The three fled from Kentucky to Michigan, then to New York, and finally to Boston, Massachusetts. The Haydens became abolitionists and helped other runaway slaves.

Anthony Burns, a 20-year-old slave, hid on a ship in Virginia that sailed to Massachusetts. In Massachusetts, Burns worked in a clothing store for a short time. He was captured as a runaway and held in a federal courthouse. The Reverend Leonard A. Grimes convinced Burns to fight for his freedom in court.

Abolitionists attacked the courthouse to free Burns. They killed one policeman, but did not free Burns. Grimes and his congregation raised $1,200 to buy freedom for Burns. But Burns lost his case against the Fugitive Slave Law.

Burns was returned to Virginia and was held in a Richmond slave jail for five months. Grimes finally bought Burns' freedom. The former slave returned to the North and became an antislavery speaker. In 1860, he settled in St. Catherines, Ontario, Canada.

Robert Smalls

In 1839, Robert Smalls was born a slave in Beaufort, South Carolina. Smalls was trained as a steamboat pilot. In May 1862, Smalls and 12 other slaves stole the Confederate supply steamboat *Planter*. The group guided the vessel out of Charleston harbor to reach Union ships blocking the harbor. For such bravery, Smalls and everyone on the ship were freed.

Conductors

Harriet Tubman was the most famous Underground Railroad conductor. She was born about 1820 to slave parents in Maryland. In 1849, she escaped to freedom in Philadelphia by following the North Star. During the 1850s, she made 19 trips into slave states. She led about 300 fugitives to freedom. Harriet Tubman also led her parents to freedom.

Tubman insisted on strict rules for trips to the North. She often forced scared or tired passengers to continue ahead with a loaded pistol.

Thomas Garrett was a Quaker from Delaware. He helped 2,700 runaways on the Underground Railroad. At age 60, he was placed on trial for helping slaves escape. The judge fined Garrett $8,000, which was all the money he had. Garrett told the judge he would continue to help runaways.

Alexander Ross was a white doctor in Belleville, Ontario, Canada. He often traveled to the Southern states to watch birds. Actually, he was a conductor for the Underground Railroad. He helped many slaves escape by giving them supplies and directions to Canada.

Harriet Tubman is perhaps the best known of all the Underground Railroad conductors. She helped more than 300 runaway slaves escape to freedom.

Chapter Six

The Underground Railroad Ends

By 1860, many states had passed laws for or against slavery. That same year, Abraham Lincoln was elected U.S. president. He did not believe in slavery even though it was legal under the U.S. Constitution. He thought the federal government had no power to outlaw slavery. He said that each state could decide for itself whether slavery was legal.

Many Southerners believed Lincoln would change his mind about slavery. They feared he might try to force states to change their laws, and ban slavery. Southern states felt that the federal government should not have that power.

On December 20, 1860, South Carolina seceded from the United States. Ten other states soon joined South Carolina in formally withdrawing from the Union. They formed a new country called the

Newspapers were filled with headlines about the Emancipation Proclamation. On January 1, 1863, this order went into effect and said slaves in the Confederate states were free.

Confederate States of America. On April 12, 1861, the Civil War between the Southern Confederacy and the Northern Union began.

On September 22, 1862, President Lincoln signed the Emancipation Proclamation. On January 1, 1863, the order went into effect. This order said all slaves in Confederate states were free. On April 9, 1865, the Civil War ended. In December 1865, the 13th amendment to the U.S. Constitution

President Lincoln and his cabinet gathered around a table for the first reading of the Emancipation Proclamation.

freed all slaves. In 1870, the U.S. Congress passed the 15th Amendment. This law gave male African Americans the right to vote.

The Underground Railroad was a dramatic protest action against slavery. This secret operation was part of organized abolitionist activity in the 1800s. The story of the Underground Railroad includes the many brave slaves determined to reach freedom, as well as the people who helped them.

TIMELINE

Slave hunters begin bringing slaves from Africa to the New World.

The American Revolution ends.

- The American Revolutionary War begins.
- The world's first abolitionist society begins.

After the War of 1812, soldiers spread the word that Canada is a safe land for runaways.

| 1500s | 1619 | 1775 | 1783 | 1793 | 1814 |

The first African indentured servants are brought to the American colonies.

The Fugitive Slave Law is passed, and the United States outlaws efforts to stop the capture of runaway slaves.

Escaped slave Frederick Douglass begins publishing the *North Star* in Rochester, New York.

President Lincoln issues the Emancipation Proclamation and orders that all slaves in Confederate territory are free. The law officially goes into effect on January 1, 1863.

Harriet Beecher Stowe's novel *Uncle Tom's Cabin* increases Northern awareness of slavery and the Underground Railroad.

- Abraham Lincoln is elected U.S. president.
- South Carolina secedes in December.

| 1847 | 1850s | 1852 | 1860 | 1861 | 1862 | 1865 |

After fleeing slavery, Harriet Tubman returns south 19 times to help rescue 300 slaves.

The Civil War begins.

- The Civil War ends.
- The 13th Amendment to the U.S. Constitution outlaws slavery.

THE LIBERATOR.

Glossary

abolition (ab-uh-LISH-shuhn)—the legal end of African American slavery

abolition society (ab-uh-LISH-shuhn suh-SYE-uh-tee)—an organization dedicated to putting an end to African American slavery

conductor (kuhn-DUHK-tur)—a person who led runaway slaves north

Confederacy (kuhn-FED-ur-uh-see)—the 11 states that left the Union were Alabama, Arkansas, Florida, Georgia, Louisiana, Mississippi, North Carolina, South Carolina, Tennessee, Texas, and Virginia

Emancipation Proclamation (i-man-si-PAY-shuhn prok-luh-MAY-shuhn)—Abraham Lincoln's order to free all slaves in Confederate held land; the Emancipation Proclamation took effect on January 1, 1863.

fugitive (FYOO-juh-tiv)—a runaway slave

Fugitive Slave Laws (FYOO-juh-tiv slayv lawz)—laws that governed the return of slaves who escaped

Quaker (KWAY-kur)—a Christian religion whose members helped runaway slaves

safe house (SAYF HOUSS)—a stop on the Underground Railroad where runaway slaves could receive food, shelter, and directions to the next stop

secede (si-SEED)—to withdraw formally from an organization

Underground Railroad (UHN-dur-ground RAYL-rohd)—an informal secret network of people who helped runaway slaves during the 1830s through the 1860s

For Further Reading

Abraham, Philip. *Harriet Tubman.* Real People. New York: Children's Press, 2002.

Ayres, Katherine. *Stealing South: A Story of the Underground Railroad.* New York: Delacorte Press, 2001.

Bentley, Judith. *"Dear Friend": Thomas Garrett & William Still, Collaborators on the Underground Railroad.* New York: Cobblehill Books, 1997.

Garrison, Mary. *Slaves Who Dared: The Stories of Ten African-American Heroes.* Shippensburg, Penn.: White Mane Kids, 2002.

Gorrel, Gena K. *North Star to Freedom: The Story of the Underground Railroad.* New York: Delacorte Press, 1997.

Heinrichs, Ann. *The Underground Railroad.* We the People. Minneapolis: Compass Point Books, 2001.

Kallen, Stuart A. *Life on the Underground Railroad.* The Way People Live. San Diego: Lucent Books, 2000.

Landau, Elaine. *Slave Narratives: The Journey to Freedom.* In Their Own Voices. New York: Franklin Watts, 2001.

Lilly, Melinda. *From Slavery to Freedom.* Reading American History. Vero Beach, Fla., Rourke, 2002.

Sawyer, Kem Knapp. *The Underground Railroad in American History.* In American History. Springfield, N.J.: Enslow Publishers, 1997.

Williams, Carla. *The Underground Railroad.* Journey to Freedom. Chanhassen, Minn.: Child's World, 2002.

Places of Interest

Harriet Tubman's House

180 South Street
Auburn, NY 13201
http://www.nyhistory.com/
harriettubman
The historic house where Harriet Tubman lived in freedom.

Hubbard House Underground Railroad Museum

P.O. Box 2666
Ashtabula, OH 44005
http://www.hubbardhouse
museum.org
This historic 19th century house displays an Underground Railroad exhibit.

National Underground Railroad Museum

Welcome Center
115 East Third Street
Marysville, KY 41056
http://www.coax.net/people/lwf/
urmuseum.htm
Life on the Underground Railroad is chronicled in this museum.

Buxton National Historic Site and Museum

North Buxton, Ontario
Canada, N0P1Y0
http://www.ciaccess.com/
~jdnewby/informat.htm
Canadian artifacts from the Underground Railroad are displayed at this museum.

Underground Railroad Museum

206 High Street
Flushing, OH 43977
http://www.ugrrf.org
Underground Railroad publications and artifacts are displayed at this museum.

Internet Sites

Do you want to learn more about The Underground Railroad?
Visit the FactHound at *http://www.facthound.com*

FactHound can track down many sites to help you. All the
FactHound sites are hand-selected by our editors. FactHound will
fetch the best, most accurate information to answer your questions.

IT'S EASY! IT'S FUN!
1) Go to *http://www.facthound.com*
2) Type in: 0736813446
3) Click on "FETCH IT" and FactHound will put you on the trail
   of several helpful links.

You can also search by subject or book title. So, relax
and let our pal FactHound do the research for you!

Index